PLATE 1

PLATE 2

slash on dotted line—insert head into opening

slash on dotted line—insert head into opening

PLATE 3

PLATE 4

cut out

PLATE 5

PLATE 6

cut on dotted line—fit flap behind head

PLATE 7

PLATE 8

cut on dotted line—fit flap behind head

CHEF

PLATE 9

cut on dotted line—fit flap behind
head

PLATE 10

poke holes through dots with a pin, run a
piece of thread through each hole and knot
on wrong side; slash on dotted line, insert
head into opening, then tie thread in a bow
under George's chin

PLATE 11

cut on dotted line—fit flap behind head

PLATE 12

slash on dotted line—insert head into opening

PLATE 13

PLATE 14

cut on dotted line—fit flap behind
head

cut on dotted line—fit flap behind
head

PLATE 15

PLATE 16